101 Things I Learned in Law School

101 Things I Learned® in Law School

Vibeke Norgaard Martin with Matthew Frederick

GRAND CENTRAL
PUBLISHING

NEW YORK   BOSTON

Matthew Frederick is the series creator, editor, and illustrator.

Grand Central Publishing
Hachette Book Group
237 Park Avenue
New York, NY 10017
www.HachetteBookGroup.com

Printed in China
QUAL

First Edition: May 2013
10 9 8 7 6 5 4 3 2 1

Grand Central Publishing is a division of Hachette Book Group, Inc.
The Grand Central Publishing name and logo is a trademark of Hachette Book Group, Inc.

The Hachette Speakers Bureau provides a wide range of authors for speaking events. To find out more, go to www.hachettespeakersbureau.com or call (866) 376-6591.

The publisher is not responsible for websites (or their content) that are not owned by the publisher.

Library of Congress Cataloging-in-Publication Data
Martin, Vibeke Norgaard.
  101 things I learned in law school / Vibeke Norgaard Martin with Matthew Frederick ; illustrations by Matthew Frederick.
     pages cm
  Includes bibliographical references and index.
  ISBN 978-1-4555-0980-5 (hardcover) — ISBN 978-1-4555-0981-2 (ebook) 1. Law—United States—Outlines, syllabi, etc. I. Frederick, Matthew, illustrator. II. Title.
  KF387.M34 2013
  349.73—dc23
                                                                                        2012040711

From Vibeke
To my two dear daughters
May you always continue to ask the questions.

Author's Note

While this book was being written, a prominent public official was charged with sexually assaulting a chambermaid in his hotel room. The official claimed the maid had initiated the encounter. Famous defense lawyer Alan Dershowitz, in presenting a mock closing argument to a trial advocacy class at Harvard Law School, attacked the defense's position. He suggested showing the jury a photograph of a naked, slightly overweight, and hunched sixty-two year-old man. The defense, Dershowitz argued to his audience, would like the court to believe that the attractive thirty-two year-old maid set her eyes upon the defendant and "simply couldn't control herself."

Dershowitz, to laughter from his audience, was using an old truth we lawyers know but do not pay enough attention to: a picture is worth a thousand words. Lawyers are word people. Take words from us and you take away our most important tool. We need words to argue, parse, and issue nuanced interpretations of complex legal concepts. But images should not be ignored, for they often provide access to concepts that words alone cannot impart with the same impact and economy.

For this reason and others, I jumped at the opportunity to create an illustrated, introductory book on the law. When I was a beginning law student, I often felt frozen by the knowledge that I knew nothing. The other students seemed to know much more than me. They bandied about terms I didn't understand and projected a confidence I lacked. Often, I found myself wanting to chuck it all and do something else. (I recall telling a fellow student that I wished I had instead followed my earlier dream to become a veterinarian, even though it would have meant putting lots of puppies to sleep.) I was sure I was the reason I had trouble understanding what my professors and fellow students were talking about.

When I started working at a large law firm, I experienced these feelings again. But with experience in practice as well as in teaching, I came to realize that there is a certain amount of posturing in the field. Law is a sink or swim environment, and posturing is a way of intimidating those who are not inclined to hide what they don't know. But the likelihood, I have learned, is that the super-confident partner, professor, or law student may be as confused and intimidated by the complexities of law as I was. This book is for them, and for anyone else looking for a starting point to explore the complex questions of the law—and who would prefer to not wade through 101,000 words.

Vibeke Norgaard Martin

Acknowledgments

From Vibeke

Thanks to Dale Barnes, Michael Bowen, Susanne Caballero, Mike Clough, Ellen Gilmore, Ben Goldstone, Ian Martin, Joe Mastro, Daniel Meyers, Amy Roach, Bob Sims, and Peter Jaszi.

From Matt

Thanks to Karen Andrews, Erik Bodenhofer, Nicole Bond, Ken Collier, Sorche Fairbank, Meredith Haggerty, Laura Hankin, Dylan Hoke, Jamie Raab, Rekha Ramani, Kallie Shimek, Nick Small, Flag Tonuzi, Tom Whatley, Rick Wolff, and Bruce Yandle.

101 Things I Learned in Law School

Year 1
Scare you to death

Year 2
Work you to death

Year 3
Bore you to death

A popular characterization of the goals of law school

Law school doesn't teach laws.

One attends law school to learn how to think like a lawyer, not to memorize laws. Laws change; how they are properly analyzed does not.

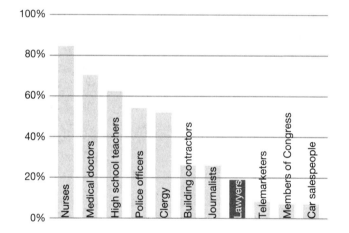

Percentage of citizens rating honesty and ethical
standards of professionals as "very high" to "high"

Lawyers must be honest, but they don't have to be truthful.

Honesty and truthfulness are not the same thing. Being honest means not telling lies. Being truthful means actively making known the full truth of a matter. Lawyers must be honest, but they do not have to be truthful. A criminal defense lawyer, for example, in zealously defending a client, has no obligation to actively present the truth. Counsel may not deliberately mislead the court, but has no obligation to tell the defendant's whole story.

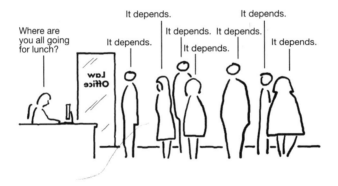

Lawyers are contextualists.

con·tex·tu·al·ist / kəhn–TEKS–choo–ə–list / *n. (pl. –ists)* a person who believes that the full meaning of a thing is not inherent in that thing, but depends on its relationship to other things.

Esquire	**Attorney**	**Lawyer**	**Solicitor**	**Barrister**

a member of the landed gentry; no formal meaning in the U.S.	anyone legally empowered to represent another, e.g., with "power of attorney"	one who is formally a member of the legal profession	(outside U.S.) performs legal work for clients outside of a trial	(outside U.S.) a specialist in court-room advocacy; usually hired by a solicitor

You're not a lawyer until you pass the bar.

The "bar" can refer to the entire legal profession, a formal portion of it, or the bar exam itself. Each state court system, federal court, and the U.S. Supreme Court is a separate bar with its own standards of admission and practice.

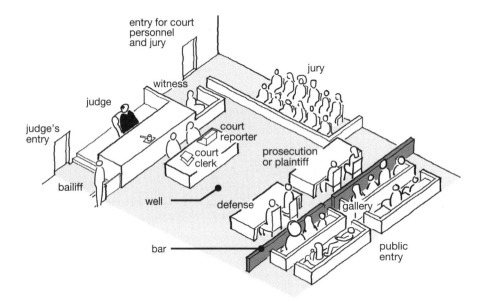

entry for court personnel and jury

jury

witness

judge

judge's entry

court reporter

court clerk

prosecution or plaintiff

bailiff

well

defense

gallery

bar

public entry

You can't pass the bar until you're a lawyer.

A courtroom is divided into two parts by a railing or similar barrier called the **bar**. Only lawyers, their clients, and witnesses who are called to testify may traverse it. The use of "bar" to refer to the legal profession as a whole derives from the tradition of barring non-participants from the trial area of the courtroom.

Systems of law in the Americas

Common law
Civil law
Hybrid

All U.S. states except Louisiana have a primary heritage in English law.

In **civil law nations**, the main source of law is legislation, and courts are bound by statutes. Courts in **common law nations** are also generally bound by statutes, but more significantly they create new law—called **common law** or **case law**—through their decisions in specific cases. They also have the power to find a statute unconstitutional.

Common law system	Civil law system
Origin in 12th century England	Origin in Holy Roman Empire
Common in English-speaking countries and former British colonies	Common in Continental Europe and its former colonies
Adversarial	Inquisitorial
Judge as arbiter: reads and interprets existing law, including that established by prior cases, but also creates new law	Judge as expert: investigates case, reads and applies existing statutes as thought fit
Law applied specific to general: an individual court case can become a more general precedent for subsequent cases	Law applied general to specific: an individual court case is subject to statutes and is not precedential
Relies on "common sense"	Presumes the state to be sensible
Flexible and generally predictable	Favors predictability over flexibility

Common law ≪ ---------------------------------- ≫ Civil law

In global context

Civil law ≪ --- ≫ Criminal law

Within common law context

"Civil law" means two things.

In the global context, civil law and common law are two primary legal systems. Within common law systems, **civil law** addresses non-criminal matters—individuals' wrongs against each other. **Criminal law** addresses individuals' wrongs against society.

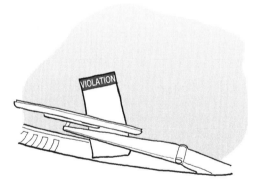

In the U.S., minor court matters are often adjudicated inquisitorially.

"Adversarial" isn't necessarily bad.

The U.S. legal system, as in most common law nations, is **adversarial**: two sides, typically represented by expert advocates, argue their positions to the court. A trial judge does not have power to investigate a case directly and usually questions witnesses only when there is a need to clarify confusing testimony.

In an **inquisitorial** system, a judge or group of judges directly investigates a case and questions litigants. Civil law nations typically employ inquisitorial procedures.

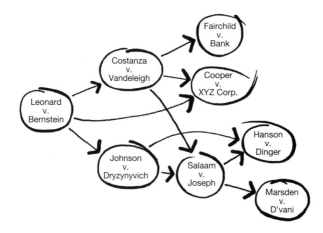

A legal ruling is the beginning, not the end, of the life of the law.

A court decision may conclude a given case, but the **precedent system** on which U.S. courts are based means a court decision is itself considered law, and it is likely to affect a line of cases far into the future. *Stare decisis*—the requirement that each court stand by previous decisions made by it and by higher courts in its jurisdiction—ensures that the law is predictable, that similar acts are adjudicated similarly, and that the consequences of a given action are known.

Constitutions

Court decisions

Statutes

Executive action

Regulations

Primary sources of law

Find one good case.

Legal argument must be supported by **primary sources of law**. If unsure where to begin research, start with **secondary sources**—legal dictionaries and encyclopedias, hornbooks (treatises on an area of the law), practice guides, and law review articles. These will provide an overview of your research topic and usually reference primary sources, including legal precedents. Once a useful precedent has been identified, almost every case that subsequently cited it can be identified by entering the case into an online citator service such as Westlaw's Keycite or Lexis's Shepherds.

With regards to Bob Berring

Lawyers are incrementalists.

Even the most inventive, aggressive, and original legal argument is constructed upon that which came before—prior court cases, constitutions, and existing statutes and regulations. This may seem limiting, but ultimately it is freeing, for the legal arena presents an opportunity found in few professional settings: to walk others down your argument path one step at a time, without interruption, from an established starting point.

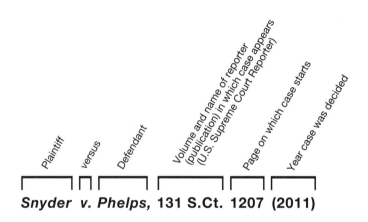

In arguing before a California court, one may cite an unpublished case from Texas, but not an unpublished case from California.

Some, but not all, court decisions are published by the court in official **court reporters**. The United States Supreme Court publishes all of its decisions, but some federal courts of appeal publish less than 10% of their decisions. Unpublished decisions generally cannot be used as a basis for argument in the same jurisdiction, although one sometimes may cite an unpublished decision from another jurisdiction as a persuasive authority.

High court

Intermediate (appeals) court

Trial court

The three-tiered court system

An appeal to an intermediate court is a right. An appeal to a court of last resort is a request.

Trial courts are the primary venues for criminal and civil cases. A litigant dissatisfied with a decision almost always has the right to appeal to an intermediate court.

Intermediate, or appellate, courts typically review a lower court's reasoning and judgment upon appeal by a litigant from a trial court case, and decide whether the trial judge properly applied the law. In some instances, the intermediate court may review the lower court's reasoning and fact-finding.

High courts consist of a panel of judges who usually decide which cases they will hear. In some states they are obligated to hear appeals in specific types of cases, such as those involving the death penalty.

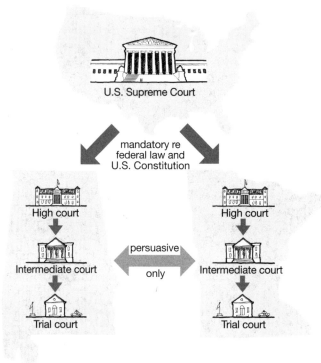

U.S. Supreme Court

mandatory re
federal law and
U.S. Constitution

High court

Intermediate court

persuasive

only

Trial court

High court

Intermediate court

Trial court

An Alabama Supreme Court case is not mandatory authority in a Minnesota court.

A state's highest court is typically bound by (1) its own previous decisions; and (2) previous decisions of the U.S. Supreme Court in matters involving federal law and the U.S. Constitution.

A state intermediate (appeals) court is typically bound by (1) its own previous decisions; (2) previous decisions of that state's high court; (3) previous decisions of the U.S. Supreme Court in matters involving federal law and the U.S. Constitution.

A state trial court is typically bound by (1) its own previous decisions; (2) previous decisions of the intermediate state court for the region the trial court is in; (3) previous decisions of the state's high court; (4) previous decisions of the U.S. Supreme Court in matters involving federal law and the U.S. Constitution.

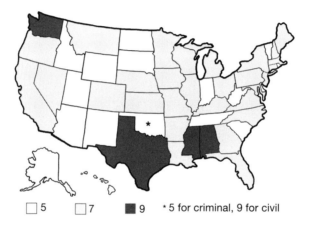

5   7   9   * 5 for criminal, 9 for civil

Number of State Supreme Court justices

A Supreme Court might be the lowest court.

Nomenclature in state court systems is not quite universal. Trial courts may be known as circuit courts, superior courts, and courts of common pleas. In California and some other states, the intermediate court is the Court of Appeals. In Maryland it is the Court of Special Appeals and the highest court is the Court of Appeals. In New York, the highest court is the Court of Appeals while lowest court is the Supreme Court.

Texas and Oklahoma each have two courts of last resort—a Supreme Court for civil cases and a Court of Criminal Appeals for criminal cases.

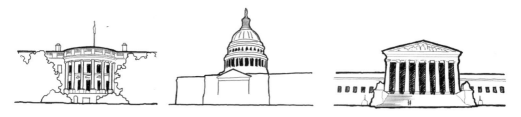

Executive branch
limited power to create law
through proclamations and
executive orders

Legislative branch
creates law by
enacting statutes

Judicial branch
creates law through
decisions made in
disputes brought to it

Requirement of a controversy

U.S. courts don't only follow existing law, but have the power to create new law and to declare existing laws unconstitutional. However, the judiciary's power to overrule the other branches of government is checked by a requirement that it act only on specific controversies brought to it. Decisions of the court are law, but the court may not actively initiate new laws.

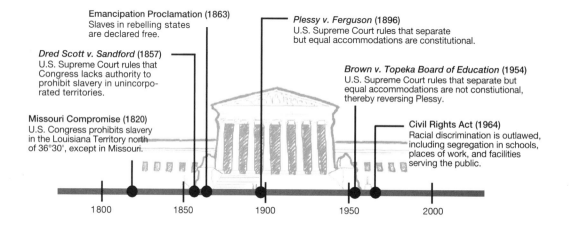

Emancipation Proclamation (1863)
Slaves in rebelling states
are declared free.

Dred Scott v. Sandford (1857)
U.S. Supreme Court rules that
Congress lacks authority to
prohibit slavery in unincorpo-
rated territories.

Missouri Compromise (1820)
U.S. Congress prohibits slavery
in the Louisiana Territory north
of 36°30', except in Missouri.

Plessy v. Ferguson (1896)
U.S. Supreme Court rules that separate
but equal accommodations are constitutional.

Brown v. Topeka Board of Education (1954)
U.S. Supreme Court rules that separate but
equal accommodations are not constiutional,
thereby reversing Plessy.

Civil Rights Act (1964)
Racial discrimination is outlawed,
including segregation in schools,
places of work, and facilities
serving the public.

1800   1850   1900   1950   2000

Sometimes the U.S. Supreme Court overrules the U.S. Supreme Court.

As society advances, discrepancies can become apparent between the law established by court precedents and more universal notions of justice. This can lead to a court reversing its previous decisions. However, when a court "reverses itself," it doesn't rewrite its earlier decision. Rather, it makes a decision in a new case that contradicts its earlier decision, thereby overruling the precedent and establishing a new precedent.

18

"There is no doubt that if there were a super-Supreme Court, a substantial proportion of our reversals of state courts would also be reversed. We are not final because we are infallible, but we are infallible only because we are final."

—ROBERT H. JACKSON
United States Supreme Court Associate Justice, 1941–1954

Attorney Thurgood Marshall, who represented the plaintiffs, became the first African American U.S. Supreme Court Justice in 1967.

Brown v. Board of Education of Topeka, 347 U.S. 483 (1954)

After the Emancipation Proclamation in 1863, policies throughout much of the U.S. supported racial segregation. In *Plessy v. Ferguson*, 163 U.S. 537 (1896), the U.S. Supreme Court ruled that separate facilities for black Americans were acceptable and afforded equal protection under the 14th Amendment.

In 1951, a group of parents of African American schoolchildren filed suit in federal court against the Topeka, Kansas Board of Education, asserting that segregation provided an inferior education. The court ruled against the plaintiffs, holding that black and white schools in Topeka were equal in all regards.

On appeal by the plaintiffs, the U.S. Supreme Court ruled 9-0 that state laws establishing separate schools for black and white students were unconstitutional, thereby reversing its earlier decision in *Plessy*. The court cited several secondary sources in its decision, including:

- Gunnar Myrdal's *An American Dilemma: The Negro Problem and Modern Democracy* (1944).
- Doll test studies by psychologists Kenneth and Mamie Clark, who argued that segregation had a negative emotional impact on black schoolchildren.

| | | |  | | |

Small claims
suits between
private parties,
usually under
$10,000

Probate
estates of the
deceased

Traffic
minor motor
vehicle
violations

Family
divorce, alimony,
child support,
custody, adoption

Juvenile
delinquent
minors

Municipal
local
ordinances

State courts of limited jurisdiction

Federal courts have limited jurisdiction.

20

Federal Courts may hear only two types of cases:

Diversity cases, i.e., in which litigants have a diversity of citizenship (such as residents of different states) and potential damages exceed $75,000;

Federal question cases, such as those involving international treaties, the U.S. government, the U.S. Constitution, and federal statutes, and disputes between states.

States also have courts of limited jurisdiction, sometimes referred to as special courts. Most cases are heard by a judge rather than jury. Courts of general jurisdiction sometimes hear appeals from courts of limited jurisdiction.

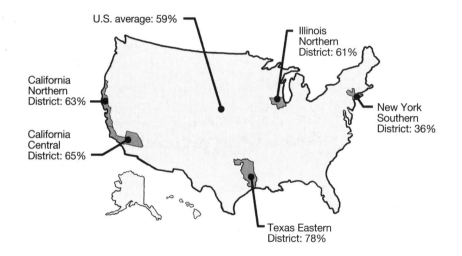

Patentee victory rates in federal patent infringement claims, 1991–2006

Erie Railroad Co. v. Tompkins, 304 U.S. 64 (1938)

21

Harry Tompkins was walking in the dark on an Erie Railroad right-of-way in Pennsylvania. A protrusion from a passing train knocked him to the ground, where a train wheel crushed his arm. Pennsylvania law would have deemed Tompkins a trespasser and required that he show Erie had acted toward him with "wanton negligence" in order to hold it liable. But Tompkins sued in federal court in New York, where Erie was incorporated. Erie argued the federal court should apply Pennsylvania state law, but Tompkins successfully argued it should apply a more general federal standard that required he prove that Erie had acted with only "ordinary negligence."

The decision was upheld on appeal by Erie. But on its subsequent appeal to the U.S. Supreme Court, the decision was reversed, with the court stating that courts must apply the law of the state in which an incident occurs.

The decision greatly limited **forum shopping**, in which a plaintiff files suit in the venue most favorable to its claims. However, many litigants still have access to several federal courts. Some, because of the influence of the internet, are now turning to foreign courts. Defamation suits by American citizens, for example, are increasingly being filed in the United Kingdom, where laws are more favorable to plaintiffs.

Patent

Copyright

Trademark

Trade secret

Intellectual property rights

22

A copyright doesn't protect an idea.

Only the specific, tangible expression of an idea, not the idea itself, can be protected by a copyright. If a screenplay is copyrighted, this prevents others from copying or otherwise using the screenplay or significant portions of it. It doesn't prevent others from writing another screenplay or making a movie using the same or similar ideas. Although it may seem unfair that the law allows others to use your ideas, it is in the best interest of society to do so, for it encourages citizens to act on, rather than sit on, new ideas.

Insurance   Sports   Family   Marine   Land use   Arts

23

Most areas of interest have a corresponding area of law practice.

Law is a profession of specialties. Attorneys work in diverse fields including medical law, sports law, family law, art law, drug control law, water law, Native American law, prison law, media law, and dozens more.

Hire a lawyer, even if you are one.

Expertise: Lawyers are specialists. Being a good lawyer in one area of the law is rarely a satisfactory substitute for hiring a specialist who intimately knows the relevant law, unique terminology, and best expert witnesses for a particular type of case.

Objectivity: Developing an effective litigation strategy calls for viewing a case from the outside, without anger, desire for revenge, or other emotional distortions.

Showmanship: Hiring a lawyer tells the other side you are serious about your complaint, or about defending yourself against a complaint, giving you a stronger position in any settlement negotiations.

The law creates fictional characters.

25

The eggshell (thin skull) plaintiff: A defendant can be liable for a plaintiff's unforeseeable and uncommon reactions. For example, if one negligently scrapes a hemophiliac, he may be liable for all the plaintiff's injuries even though the same harm to another person would have been minor.

The fertile octogenarian: Probate law (wills, trusts, and estates) assumes a woman is capable of giving birth until she dies.

The corporation: An abstract entity that, like a person, may own property, enter into contracts, sue and be sued, be held liable under civil and criminal law, and even have some constitutional rights.

The reasonable person: An imaginary individual placed in the circumstances of a litigant or other party at the time of a given action. For example, in a negligence case, a reasonable person acts sensibly and without undue delay.

Institutions

Estates

Corporations

Infants
(via guardian)

Municipalities

Individuals

Parties that often have standing

Corporations have standing. Trees do not.

A plaintiff has **standing** if it is the proper party to request that the court hear and rule on a legal controversy. Three overlapping requirements generally must be met:

1. **The plaintiff must have suffered or is imminently likely to suffer an injury.** One cannot sue a logging company on behalf of an injured tree, or the federal government over a general objection to its misspending of monies.
2. **The defendant must be the cause of the plaintiff's injury.** A plaintiff lacks standing if its injury cannot be traced to the defendant's behavior or if it resulted through a third party not named in the suit.
3. **The injury must be redressable through the court.** A favorable ruling from the court must be likely to benefit the plaintiff. The court cannot act, for example, if the plaintiff seeks redress from a party not involved in the suit.

"A ship has a legal personality, a fiction found useful for maritime purposes.... So it should be as respects valleys, alpine meadows, rivers, lakes, estuaries, beaches, ridges, groves of trees, swampland, or even air that feels the destructive pressures of modern technology and modern life.... The voice of the inanimate object, therefore, should not be stilled."

27

—WILLIAM DOUGLAS, dissenting opinion
Sierra Club v. Morton (1972)

Denzel Washington as attorney Joe Miller in *Philadelphia* (1993)

Explain it to an eight-year-old.

The "bones" of a case—its essential facts and structure, and the argument you are making in support of your position—should be understandable in simple terms. If you can explain it to a child, you can explain it to a jury.

The theory of a case

The theory of a case is the single most plausible storyline of a litigating position. It is the core around which all points of a case are organized; the idea that remains standing should all else be taken away. It is at once a logical and emotional center: it is consistent with every piece of evidence the judge or jury will accept, and it considers the subjective positions taken by the litigants and the perspectives likely to be taken by the judge and jury. Ideally, a theory is so clearly the core of one's case that it is implicitly appended to every point one makes: "…and that is why my client…"

There should be only one theory, consisting of a few sentences, which will always tell you where you are and where you need to go when in the midst of an oral argument, deposition, or research.

30

Insight doesn't arrive head-on.

Be suspicious of the person who sizes up a new situation very quickly, claims understanding, and stakes out an ironclad position. Insight usually requires long periods of discussion, research, analysis, rationalization, and counter-argument, and it rarely arrives while attacking a matter directly or on a first pass. If one occasionally is able to quickly understand a complex matter, he or she is far more likely to quickly *mis*understand it.

"… I made three arguments in every case. First came the one I had planned—as I thought, logical, coherent, complete. Second was the one actually presented—interrupted, incoherent, disjointed, disappointing. The third was the utterly devastating argument that I thought of after going to bed that night."

31

—JUSTICE ROBERT H. JACKSON, "Advocacy Before the Supreme Court: Suggestions for Effective Case Presentations," 37 *ABA Journal* 801, 803 (1951)

An attorney may approach the witness only with the judge's permission.

Give your witnesses a home base.

It can be difficult for a witness to remain calm and composed if the opposing attorney asks questions for which the witness has not prepared, uses different wording than that expected, or asks a series of questions that leads the witness into suggesting a position he or she does not believe is true.

When preparing witnesses for trial, identify a home base from which testimony is to emerge. A home base is not a rehearsed answer, but a core position inherent in a witness's relationship to and knowledge of the case. Although it may be different for each witness, each home base grows out of and directly supports the case's central theory.

Leading questions

Non-leading questions

A hostile witness can be helpful.

33

Friendly witnesses are those called to give testimony in support of one's own case. **Hostile witnesses** are called by the opposing party. An examining attorney may ask **leading questions**—those calling for yes/no responses—only of the opposing party's witnesses. However, if a friendly witness is evasive or uncooperative, the examining attorney may request permission from the judge to treat the witness as hostile. If granted, the attorney may ask leading questions, allowing the attorney much tighter control of the examination.

Mr. Johnson, that's you on the videotape, isn't it?

Yes.

And we can all see the day and time stamp on the video, can't we?

Yes.

Yet you told the police you were in bed at that time, didn't you?

Yes.

SO YOU WERE LYING, WEREN'T YOU, YOU LOUSY #$@%&*?!

Avoid asking a question in court if you don't already know the answer.

A trial is not the time and place to be surprised by the answer to a question. It's better to be surprised during pretrial discovery.

When an answer to a question would be quite obvious and favorable to your case, it is sometimes effective to not ask it at all, and to leave the general awareness of it hanging in the courtroom air.

Ways to discredit a witness

Bias: Show that the witness is testifying under an immunity agreement or plea bargain, has a personal relationship with someone involved in the case, or is being paid for expertise.

Contradiction: Show that a witness's testimony is inconsistent with that of other witnesses or evidence, is contradicted by previous statements by the witness (e.g., deposition), or is selective or incomplete.

Character: Show that the witness has been dishonest in other statements or actions or has criminal convictions suggesting dishonesty.

Limitations: Show the witness's view was obstructed, or that witness has abnormal memory due to mental incapacity or intoxication.

Expertise: Show that credentials are inadequate or not specific to the subject, or that the purity of the evidence evaluated by the expert is in question.

Witnesses were once "suits."

Before the development of a coherent legal system in England in the 12th century, a plaintiff substantiated a claim by bringing to the local decision makers a **suit**—a group of witnesses who supported his position against a defendant. Thus a plaintiff literally "brought a suit."

Trial
a formal, evidence-based
procedure conducted in court
to determine a verdict

Hearing
a comparatively informal
administrative procedure to
determine a limited matter

Put some length in your briefs, but keep your motions short.

A **motion** is a written or oral request to the court, made before, during, or even after a legal proceeding, to rule on a specific issue, such as to disallow certain testimony, dismiss charges, or request a new trial. Motions should be kept short and simple so the court may understand what is being asked of it. The place to elaborate on a motion is in a **brief**—a persuasive written document filed with the court, setting forth one's legal and factual arguments. A brief is a lawyer's only way, other than oral presentation, of arguing to the judge.

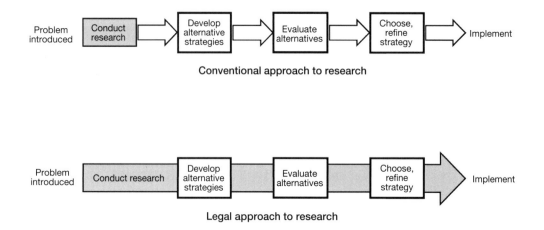

Conventional approach to research

Legal approach to research

Research isn't finished until the deadline arrives.

Research is a primary, not preliminary, activity. Through research, one finds the law that supports an argument, that may argue against it, and that may mitigate the counter-arguments. New precedents emerge constantly, up to and concurrently with the presentation of a closing argument.

With regards to Bob Berring

Issues
identify matter(s) of
concern in the
current case

Rule of law
from prior cases:
identify and explain how
it was interpreted

Application
compare facts from prior
case to current case and
apply rule of law

Conclusion
a summary that
follows naturally from
the preceding

The IRAC sequence of argument

Writing isn't recording your thoughts; it's thinking on the page.

A well-constructed argument rarely, if ever, resembles what one started with. Writing effectively isn't recording the argument one wishes to make; it is a process of discovering what one's argument needs to be. Through writing, thinking, researching, rewriting, rethinking, and rewriting again, an argument is discovered and clarified.

"Every judgment I write tells a lie against itself.... The actual journey of a judgment starts with the most tentative exploratory ideas, and passes through large swathes of doubt and contestation before finally ending up as a confident exposition purportedly excluding any possibility of error. The erratic, even contradictory pathways, are hidden."

40

—ALBIE SACHS, Former Justice,
Constitutional Court of South Africa

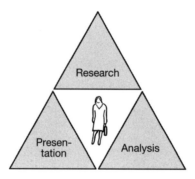

Skills for a lawyer

Good argument trumps good facts...if you're a student.

Lawyers need good facts, good law, and good arguments. Students benefit from all three, but above all must develop and demonstrate the ability to make good arguments. Whether working from good or bad facts, or good or bad law, students need to show they can use the resources they have to convincingly support or refute a position.

The Toulmin Model of Argument

Don't try to prove you are objectively right; show that your position is preferable to the alternative.

It is always possible to make at least some arguments for or against a legal position. An argument requires logic, but legal argument is not a purely logical form of argument that promises a universal, absolute conclusion. Rather, it is a practical form of argument that aims to establish one claim as more probable or reasonable than another.

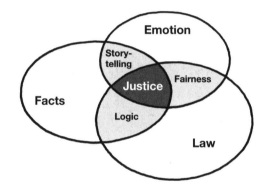

If the law is in your favor, pound the law. If the facts are in your favor, pound the facts. If neither is in your favor, pound the table.

Few judges will rule against clear precedent. When relevant law favors your position, identify it and return to it again and again. If the law does not clearly favor your argument, emphasize the facts of the case most likely to engender sympathy for your client, so the judge or jury might favorably interpret any gray areas in the law.

And on second thought, never pound the table.

Always be the most reasonable person in the room.

Lawyers are officers of the court, as are judges, bailiffs, and other court personnel. All are obligated to safeguard the proper comportment of the judicial process. Projecting that one is careful, knowledgeable, thoughtful, and considerate is more important than projecting that one is to be feared. Even if others act poorly, you cannot use it as a reason to act poorly yourself.

Caucasians are pink.
I am Caucasian.
I am pink.

Caucasians are pink.
Spam is pink.
Bubblegum is pink.
My dog's tongue is pink.
There must be other pink things.

Spam is pink.
I am pink.
I'm pink; therefore I'm Spam.

Proper deduction
premises guarantee
truth of conclusion

Proper induction
premises suggest
likely conclusion

Improper deduction
premises do not
suggest conclusion

Make a logical argument.

Deductive logic: usually works from broadly accepted truths toward demonstrating a truth in a specific situation, although more properly it is any argument in which the premises guarantee that their logical outcome is a truth.

Inductive logic: tends to work from specific examples of truth toward demonstration of a larger truth, but can be any argument whose conclusion, while not guaranteed, is a likely or highly probable outcome of the premises. Successful inductive reasoning requires a convincingly large sample size.

The defendant
mercilessly
killed his ex-wife.

Weak

The defendant aimed a rusty musket
at his wife's face and callously pulled
the trigger. The bullet entered her
skull through her right eye socket.
She died over the course of three
hours. Her children, ages 1, 3, and 7,
never saw her again.

Stronger

Tell a compelling story.

A proper argument is not driven by emotion, but if an argument lacks an emotional component it might not connect with a judge or jury. Convey facts accurately, but also set a scene so the audience can make an emotional connection to events and characters. Emotions attach to details, not to abstractions and generalities.

With regards to Bill Fernholz

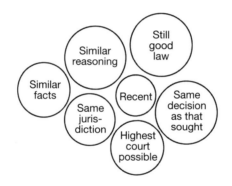

Components of a good precedent

Let your citations argue for you.

The strength of a legal argument lies in its grounding in past legal arguments that have been acknowledged in court rulings as sound. In legal writing, every sentence, other than those containing one's own thoughts and making no inference from a past case, should be followed by a citation referencing a source.

Master the transitions.

Addition: And, Also, Another reason, Besides, Equally important, Finally, Furthermore, In addition, In other words, Moreover, Next, Similarly

Alternative: Alternatively, Although, But, Contrary to, Conversely, Even though, However, In contrast, Nevertheless, On the other hand, Regardless, Still, Though, Yet

Analogy: Again, Also, Analogously, Likewise, Similarly

Introducing an example: For example, For instance, In particular, Namely, Specifically, That is

Establishing a causal consequence: As a result, Because, Consequently, It follows, Since, Then, Therefore, Thus

Signaling a concession: Although, Granted, It is true, No doubt, To be sure

To signal one is about to speak about a client's case: Here, In the case at hand, In the present matter

Concluding: Accordingly, All in all, As a result, Consequently, Finally, Hence, In short, In summary, Lastly, Therefore, Thus, To summarize

The defendant
shot the victim
and hid the gun
in his garage.

Yes, a gun was found in
the defendant's garage.
However, other events
account for this.

Active voice
indicates direct
connection

Passive voice
suggests incidental
relationship

Sometimes passive voice is stronger.

Statements made in the active voice tend to convey direct connections and are usually the more effective form of argument. Passive voice suggests incidental connections, and usually sounds weaker and less convincing. However, there are occasions when passive voice is the more effective form—such as when conveying an incidental connection is precisely one's point.

Something reasonable is reasonable, not "not unreasonable."

It's fine to *count* things; you don't have to *enumerate* them. If something happened *at that point in time*, it happened *then*. If an event occurred *as a result of the fact of x*, it occurred *because of x*. If the *alleged perpetrator was observed carrying an unidentified implement on his person in the course of events ensuing subsequent to a crime*, the *defendant carried something after a crime*.

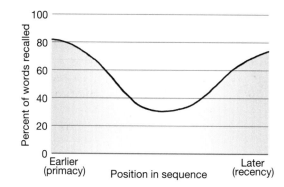

The Recency Effect

Stop talking when you've made your point.

Begin and end every argument or talking point with the thing you most want the listener to note or remember. Early points tend to be remembered because they aren't yet competing with all the others to come. As one continues to speak, each new word or idea presented to the listener competes for memory space with all the previous words and ideas.

Items at the end of a talk tend to be better remembered because they are recent in memory, and are perhaps still in the "working" portion of one's memory. Additionally, listener interest is elevated at the conclusion because it is understood as the critical summing up of previous points made—and perhaps not listened to.

51

How to misunderstand a contract

Unilateral mistake: One party is in error as to a contract's terms or subject matter. The contract usually will be upheld by the court, except courts may void or revise a contract if the non-mistaken party was aware of and tried to take advantage of the mistake, or if enforcement would be unconscionable (e.g., a very one-sided contract).

Mutual mistake: Both parties are mistaken as to the meaning of a contract term. The mistakes may be different from each other (varying interpretations of a word), or they may be the same, such as a shared misunderstanding of an external fact (e.g., "to occur on February 29, 2015"). Some courts call the former a mutual mistake and the latter a **common mistake**. Courts usually will find the contract was never formed and therefore will not enforce it.

52

The *Peerless* Case

Two businessmen, Raffles and Wichelhaus, entered into a contract for the sale of 125 bales of cotton. Shipment from India to England was scheduled to be made on the British ship *Peerless*. Unknown to both parties, there were two British ships of this name. Wichelhaus, the receiver, expected shipment on the *Peerless* arriving in October, but it was carried on the other *Peerless*, which arrived in December. Wichelhaus refused to accept delivery.

Raffles sued Wichelhaus for breach of contract, but the court was unable to ascertain which ship named *Peerless* was intended in the written agreement. As the parties did not agree to the same thing, there was no **meeting of the minds**, and therefore no binding contract. The court ruled that Wichelhaus did not have to purchase the cotton from Raffles.

The *Peerless* case, although from British law (*Raffles v Wichelhaus* [1864] EWHC Exch J19), is well-known in American law because it largely established the concept of the meeting of the minds—and likely also because of the great irony in there being two ships named *Peerless*.

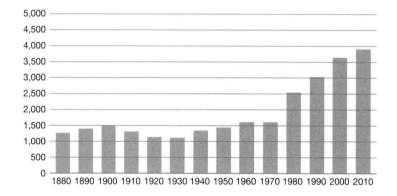

Number of lawyers in U.S. per 100,000 citizens

A lawyer may not practice law with a non-lawyer, unless the non-lawyer is in jail.

Anyone may give legal advice, but the recipient has to know if the advice is or is not coming from a lawyer. For this reason, a lawyer may not enter into a business enterprise with a non-lawyer if its activities include the practice of law. A client could become confused as to the source and reliability of advice, and whether communications with the firm are privileged. However, a lawyer is permitted to assist the legal efforts of a "jailhouse lawyer"—a prisoner who provides legal advice to other prisoners.

Damages
payment for plaintiff's
losses

**Specific performance
or injunction**
litigant must perform or cease
performing a specific act

Declaratory remedy
Rights and obligations of
litigants clarified

Some civil remedies

One cannot simply sue, but must sue for *something*.

A plaintiff must request a specific **remedy**, such as a payment it wishes the defendant to make or an action it wants the defendant to take or stop taking. A plaintiff cannot ask the court to issue an advisory opinion, make a public statement on an issue, or edit a statute.

If waiting for a final decision from the court might prove ineffectual to a plaintiff, he or she may request an **injunction**—a court order that the opposing party do or stop doing an act—at any time. The court may grant the request before a trial is completed if: (1) It deems the plaintiff likely to succeed in the case; (2) the plaintiff is likely to suffer irreparable harm if it is not granted; (3) The plaintiff will likely endure greater harm from the absence of injunction than the other party will endure from it; and (4) the injunction is in the public interest.

55

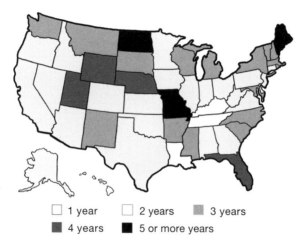

Statutes of limitations on personal injury claims

You can't sleep on your rights.

The law limits how long after an injury has occurred, or has been discovered to have occurred, that a claim or charge can be brought. A **statute of limitations** serves to provide a sense of finality and predictability for the defendant, and to make sure a claim can be resolved while evidence is available, memories are fresh, and testimony may be considered reliable.

Actual damages
an award for direct
injury or loss

Consequential damages
an award for
indirect costs

Future damages
for expected losses, e.g.,
medical expenses,
reduced income

Punitive damages
punishes defendant for
recklessness, malice, or deceit

Attorney's fees

Common civil awards

An injured party has a responsibility to minimize the damage.

In many jurisdictions, a party suffering a personal injury cannot recover for losses incurred for failing to seek reasonable medical care, unless the conduct that caused the injury was willful or done in bad faith.

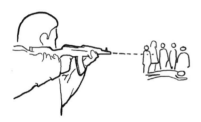

Foreseeable

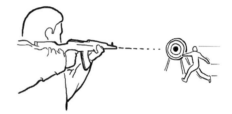

Not foreseeable

Palsgraf v. Long Island Railroad Co., 248 N.Y. 339 (1928)

A man carrying an ordinary looking package was hurrying to board a moving train. A Long Island Railroad employee helped pull the passenger into the rail car while another employee pushed. The package was dislodged and fell. Unfortunately, it contained fireworks and exploded, and the force knocked down a scale at the end of the platform, injuring a Mrs. Palsgraf.

Palsgraf sued the railroad, claiming her injury resulted from negligent acts by its employees. Palsgraf won in trial court, but on appeal by LIRR to the highest court in New York, Palsgraf's complaint was dismissed in a 4-3 vote. The court held that LIRR's conduct, if wrongful in regard to the man carrying the parcel, was not wrongful in regard to Palsgraf. Citizens have a **duty of care** and must refrain from acts that threaten the safety of others, but cannot be held liable for injurious acts if the consequences could not have been **reasonably foreseen**. Since the railroad was not given notice that the package contained dangerous fireworks, it could not foresee that Palsgraf was within a zone of danger.

Palsgraf is often cited—incorrectly—for the role of **proximate cause** in injury cases, even though the decision by the court specifically stated this was not a consideration. When there is no duty of care, causation does not matter.

Good Samaritans can be liable for negligence.

The Thin Skull Rule

When a **tort** results in harm to a person with a preexisting physical or mental condition, such that the harm is greater than what would have been experienced by a different victim, a defendant may be held liable for all such harm.

Pleading

The plaintiff files a complaint. The defendant answers, demurs, or files a cross-complaint.

Discovery and motion practice

Evidence and sworn statements are exchanged. Pretrial motions are filed.

Trial

Facts and arguments are presented before a judge or judge and jury.

The 3 stages of a civil case

Most of what happens in a civil trial happened before the trial.

In civil cases, litigants are required to exchange information before trial. Through the **discovery process**, each party may depose (question under oath) the opposition and any other individuals who may provide relevant information. Consequently, each side knows the other's case well before the trial begins.

A judge is also involved well before trial. A judge reads pretrial pleadings and motions from the two sides, researches relevant legal issues, settles disputes that arise during discovery, issues warrants and summonses, and supervises jury selection. Most cases settle before trial, making pretrial work the court's main work.

No insanity defense, but allows verdict of "guilty but insane" or "guilty but mentally ill"

No insanity defense

States not allowing an insanity defense

The party that alleges bears the burden of proof.

Each party in a dispute bears the burden of proving its allegations. A party that denies an allegation, with few exceptions, has no obligation to disprove it. However, if a criminal defendant enters a plea of **not guilty by reason of insanity**, thereby conceding to the prosecution's charge, it inherits a burden of proving insanity.

In a very few civil disputes, the defendant bears the burden of proof. For example, a customer sued by a utility provider for nonpayment may have to prove to the court that the bill was paid or provide a convincing justification for why it was not.

61

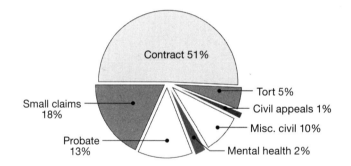

State civil court cases

The party that alleges gets an extra chance to argue its case.

Opening statements: The plaintiff or prosecutor presents an initial summary of its case, and the opposing party follows.

Plaintiff/prosecutor's case-in-chief: The plaintiff/prosecutor calls its witnesses for direct examination. After each examination, the defense may conduct a cross-examination. The plaintiff/prosecutor may then re-question each witness regarding matters that emerged from the cross-examination.

Defendant's case-in-chief: The defense calls its witnesses for direct examination. After each examination, the plaintiff/prosecution may conduct a cross examination. The defense may re-question each witness to address matters that emerged from the cross-examination.

Rebuttal case: The plaintiff/prosecutor may request to proceed with rebuttal evidence in response to the defendant's case-in-chief. The judge may allow the defendant to rebut the plaintiff/prosecutor's rebuttal if it introduced new matters.

When either side completes its case-in-chief, defense, or rebuttal, it will indicate that it rests. Counsel may reopen a closed phase of the trial only with permission.

Closing arguments: Plaintiff/prosecutor; defendant; then plaintiff/prosecutor.

Deliberations and verdict.

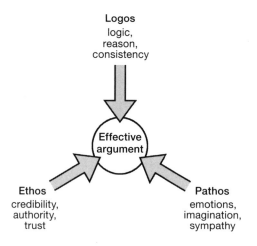

Keep it slightly above room temperature.

Rationality is cool; passion is warm. Rationality provides logical justification for a position, while passion provides a human connection to it. Both are needed to advance an argument; an abundance of one will not compensate for a dearth of the other. An argument may be extraordinarily rational, but its correctness alone is unlikely to compel others to care enough to right the wrongs behind it. An extremely passionate argument may initially attract sympathy, but unmitigated displays of emotion at the expense of rationality will wear thin and eventually prompt others to tune out your message.

Rationality makes an argument worthy. Passion makes it worthwhile.

What's in dispute—facts or law?

Law: A statute requires a paroled sex offender to live at least 2,000 feet from a school.

Facts: The parolee already owns a home less than 2,000 feet from a school, and nearly all other residences in the community are similarly sited.

Question for the court: Is a law constitutional if it promotes a parolee's homelessness?

Law: The vehicle code requires motorists to stop at red lights.

Facts: A police officer cited the defendant for running a red light. The defendant says the light was red, but that he went through it to make way for a fire truck.

Question for the court: Was the defendant making way for an emergency vehicle, and does this mean he should be excused for running the red light?

64

Law: A contract requires both parties to have the same understanding of its critical terms.

Facts: Party A agreed to purchase all of Party B's bats. Party B delivered a cage of live bats to the buyer, who was expecting sports equipment.

Question for the court: Did one party or the other conceal its awareness of the other's misunderstanding at the time of contract?

Laws regulating
individual conduct

Laws providing for
state services

Laws empowering
or directing local
governments

Laws determining
raising and spend-
ing of money

Amendments
to the state
constitution

Five categories of statutes in the state of North Carolina

When meaning is contested, look to intent.

When the meaning of a statute is disputed, courts look to legislative intent (the policy and broader legislative scheme behind it); language (composition, structure, qualifying words, technical versus general meaning); and history (events leading to and following the legislation).

When the meaning of a contract term is disputed, courts generally look to what the parties intended when they entered into the contract. If a specific word is in dispute, courts usually presume the generally accepted meaning unless one party can prove that a narrower or more specialized meaning is its proper interpretation.

65

Zealous advocacy
for client, within
legal bounds

Loyalty
cannot assume a position
adverse to client's interest

Confidentiality
must maintain confidences of
clients and potential clients

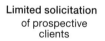

Limited solicitation
of prospective
clients

Competence
must have appropriate skills,
time, and qualifications

Communication
must keep client
well informed

Ethics for lawyers

A lawyer may not reveal that a client intends to commit a crime.

A client's communications to his attorney are protected by rules of confidentiality and the **attorney-client privilege**, except when the attorney believes the crime will result in death, severe bodily harm, or (in some jurisdictions) substantial financial injury. However, a lawyer must make a good faith effort to dissuade a client from committing a crime and has no responsibility to maintain confidentiality if the client hired the lawyer specifically for assistance in committing it.

Noncoincident political and cultural boundaries

4 types of boundaries

Political boundaries define sovereign or locally sovereign entities such as cities, counties, states, and nations. They result from numerous, often competing factors, such as geography, culture, long-term settlement patterns, conquest, and negotiation.

Electoral boundaries establish voting areas for legislative bodies. They are generally coincident with political boundaries, but may change with relative frequency to coordinate elective representation with population shifts.

Jurisdictional boundaries define regions administered by court systems and law enforcement agencies. They typically coincide with political boundaries.

Cultural boundaries demarcate regions in which the inhabitants' language, customs, and other social practices differ from those of surrounding areas. Cultural boundaries are often independent of other types of boundaries.

Navajo Nation is larger than ten states.

There are more than 300 nations within the United States.

The U.S. Constitution grants **local sovereignty** to over 300 American Indian reservations. They cannot enter into treaties with foreign entities, but Indian nations have their own court systems, which adjudicate matters involving Indian affairs on tribal land. They cannot adjudicate matters involving non-Indians.

68

Jails

run by sheriffs or local governments;
house inmates awaiting trial or
convicts serving short sentences

Prisons

run by state or federal governments;
detain individuals serving longer
sentences for serious crimes

Felonies, misdemeanors, and wobblers

Felony: a serious crime, usually punishable by imprisonment for more than one year. Includes arson, assault, battery, burglary, grand larceny, grand theft, multiple offense DUI, murder, rape, robbery, serious drug offenses, unauthorized possession of a deadly weapon, and vandalism of federal property.

Misdemeanor: a crime less serious than a felony, usually punishable by a fine, forfeiture, or less than a year in prison or jail. Typically includes disorderly conduct, first offense DUI, possession of small amounts of some drugs, petty theft, prostitution, public intoxication, reckless driving, simple assault, trespassing, and vandalism.

Wobbler: a crime that can be charged as a felony or misdemeanor depending on circumstance; for example, if there is an aggravating factor. Some felonies may be reduced to misdemeanors during sentencing or even after conviction.

	State crimes	**Federal crimes**
Pretrial Discovery	Required early in proceedings, long before trial	Occurs much later; prosecutor not required to provide witness statements until after witness has testified.
Sentencing	Mandatory minimums for some crimes, but a judge may be lenient in unusual circumstances.	Severe mandatory minimums based on the offense and defendant's criminal history.

If you're going to spray graffiti, don't do it on the Post Office.

Crimes typically prosecuted in state court

Assault and battery
Domestic violence
Embezzlement
Fraud
Murder
Most misdemeanors
Operating under the influence
Possession of controlled
  substances
Rape/sex crimes/child molestation
Robbery/theft
Trafficking in controlled substances
  not crossing state lines

Crimes typically prosecuted in federal court

Bank robbery/bank fraud
Bribery of public officials/public
  corruption
Child pornography
Crimes committed on federal property
Crimes involving state to state flight
Export crimes
Mail and wire fraud/theft
Money laundering
Securities fraud
Tax crimes
Trafficking in controlled substances
  across state or federal lines

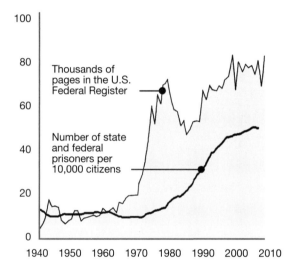

Thousands of pages in the U.S. Federal Register

Number of state and federal prisoners per 10,000 citizens

"The more laws and order are made prominent, the more thieves and robbers there will be."

—LAO-TZU

Just don't
inhale.

You're allowed to puff.

If you are selling something and you fudge a little, it's ok. You're allowed to exaggerate how good something is in an effort to make a sale, as long as you are expressing an opinion and not misrepresenting a fact. Some **puffing** is expected of any salesperson.

72

	Involuntary manslaughter	Voluntary manslaughter	Second degree murder	First degree murder
Did killer intend to kill?	No	Sometimes	Usually	Yes
Did killing result from negligence?	Yes	No	No	No
Was killing premeditated?	No	No	No	Yes
Was killing result of "heat of passion"?	N.A.	Sometimes	Sometimes	N.A.

Common homicide standards

Intent can be essential; motive rarely is.

Motive is the reason someone has for committing a crime. It can help the prosecution identify and indict a defendant, but it doesn't provide direct evidence of guilt. Personal financial difficulty, for example, could suggest an individual had a motive to commit a robbery, but it provides, at best, only circumstantial evidence that he did so.

Intent is the resolution to commit a crime. A defendant's possession of tools for breaking a safe suggests an intent to commit burglary and theft, and may serve as direct evidence of his guilt.

Motive is not essential to the court when guilt is clearly established by the evidence. But if the prosecution's case is based largely on circumstantial evidence, motive might be a persuasive consideration—for either guilt or innocence.

73

 +  =

Guilty act + guilty mind = Guilty

Actus non facit reum nisi mens sit rea means "an act does not make one guilty unless his mind is also guilty." For a defendant to be found guilty of most crimes, he must have some awareness that his act was criminal.

When a defendant enters a plea of not guilty by reason of insanity, he is arguing he lacked *mens rea*—the capacity to appreciate why his actions were wrong. In some states, an insanity plea allows an "irresistible impulse" defense, which says the defendant understood his behavior was wrong but was unable to control it.

In civil cases, a defendant can be held liable without demonstration of a *mens rea*. But if it is successfully demonstrated, the award for damages is often increased.

74

General deterrence

discouraging criminal acts through public displays of punishment

Specific deterrence

reducing offenders' ability to commit future crimes through incarceration/incapacitation

Rehabilitation

reducing future crimes by helping offenders become productive

Retribution

discouraging crime by issuing punishment in proportion to severity

Watchful eye

reducing crime through fear or embarrassment of being caught

Broken window theory

discouraging aggressive crime patterns by repairing evidence of small infractions

Crime deterrence

A criminal defendant may have to conduct a criminal investigation.

Unlike civil litigants, who are entitled to acquire sworn, pretrial statements from the opposing side through the discovery process, a criminal defendant does not usually have the right to interview the prosecution or its witnesses. Consequently, a trial is usually a criminal defense attorney's first opportunity to question the prosecution's witnesses.

The prosecution is required, however, to provide the defense a list of its witnesses as well as any potentially exculpatory evidence it possesses. Otherwise, a criminal defendant and/or his attorney often have to hire a private investigator to identify evidence and witnesses to support his case.

75

Hourly fee
usually billed in 1/10 hr.
increments

Contingency fee
percentage of award
to client

Flat fee
payable regardless
of outcome

Contingency fees are prohibited in criminal cases.

A contingency fee is payable to an attorney only upon the successful outcome of a civil case. In a criminal case, a contingency fee could create a conflict of interest—for example, in a murder case in which the defendant is the named beneficiary of the victim's life insurance policy. If the defense attorney's fee was based on the policy payout, she would not get paid if the defendant pleaded guilty via a plea bargain, and thereby would have no incentive to plea bargain on behalf of the client—even if it was in her client's best interest.

76

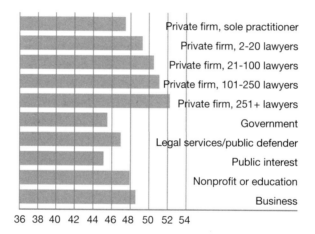

	Private firm, sole practitioner
	Private firm, 2-20 lawyers
	Private firm, 21-100 lawyers
	Private firm, 101-250 lawyers
	Private firm, 251+ lawyers
	Government
	Legal services/public defender
	Public interest
	Nonprofit or education
	Business

36 38 40 42 44 46 48 50 52 54

Answer to question, "How many hours did you work last week?"

An hour can be 116 minutes long.

Lawyers usually bill in 6-minute (1/10 hour) increments. A 3.1-minute phone conversation could result in a bill for 6 minutes.

77

Invoking the Fifth Amendment in a criminal trial prevents self-incrimination. Invoking it in a civil trial may *induce* self-incrimination.

Amendment V to the U.S. Constitution grants citizens accused of a crime the right to remain silent to avoid incriminating themselves. Witnesses in a civil trial may invoke this right only if a statement might implicate them in a crime for which prosecution is possible. The court and jury are usually entitled to make an **adverse inference** against a civil witness who does so.

78

Spousal

Academic research

Reporter

Psychotherapeutic

Clergy-communicant

Congressional

Informer

Executive

Common privileges

If a client brings a friend to a meeting with an attorney, privilege might be lost.

The attorney-client privilege forbids a lawyer from disclosing information about a client's case to anyone without the client's permission. An attorney usually cannot be forced to reveal such information even in a legal proceeding. However, if a client brings a third party to a meeting with her attorney, and that party is not there to further her interest, the privilege may be lost.

79

You don't know the rule until you know the exceptions.

A presumption of all court testimony is that the opposing side may cross-examine its source. If a witness quotes someone who is not available for cross examination, the statement, if objected to by the opposing attorney, might be ruled **hearsay** and be forbidden.

The rule against hearsay testimony has about thirty exceptions. In order to get a statement made outside court into court when its originator is unavailable to testify, one has to determine how to fit it into at least one of the exceptions. In practice, the exceptions to the rule are the rule.

80

Direct evidence   Circumstantial evidence

Circumstantial evidence can be more damning than direct evidence.

Direct evidence supports an assertion without need for other evidence or inferences. Eyewitness testimony is a common form of direct evidence: "I saw the defendant stab the victim" directly supports the prosecution's case against a defendant.

Circumstantial evidence has more than one possible interpretation, and therefore must be connected to other evidence or inferences to support an assertion. "I saw the defendant enter the building" does not indicate a defendant's direct connection to a crime. But if multiple sources provide related testimony such that each checks and reinforces the others, a convincing argument may be made. By contrast, a single instance of direct eyewitness testimony may be mistaken or driven by ulterior motives.

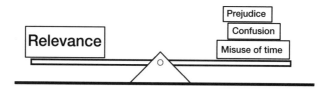

Useful evidence isn't necessarily admissible evidence.

Relevance: Is the evidence connected to the issues at trial? Will it make an important alleged fact in the case more or less probable?

Authentication: Can the evidence be shown to be what its proponent says it is? Can a proper chain of custody be shown, for example, by bringing to court the police officer who found it?

Hearsay: If the source of the evidence cannot appear in court, can the evidence be admitted under a hearsay exception?

Privileges: Will any privileges (spousal, attorney-client, etc.) prevent the evidence from being admitted?

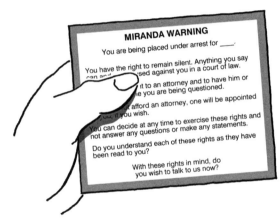

MIRANDA WARNING

You are being placed under arrest for ____.

You have the right to remain silent. Anything you say can and ____ used against you in a court of law.

____ it to an attorney and to have him or ____ne you are being questioned.

____ afford an attorney, one will be appointed ____ou, if you wish.

You can decide at any time to exercise these rights and not answer any questions or make any statements.

Do you understand each of these rights as they have been read to you?

With these rights in mind, do you wish to talk to us now?

Miranda v. Arizona, 384 U.S. 436 (1966)

A few days before his twenty-second birthday in 1963, Ernesto Miranda was arrested in Arizona for kidnapping and rape. After a two-hour police interrogation, Miranda, who had a history of mental instability, signed a confession that was later used against him at trial. His court-appointed attorney objected to the confession's use at trial, arguing that the police had not properly informed Miranda of his rights to counsel and to remain silent, making the confession less than voluntary. The objection was overruled, and Miranda was found guilty.

Miranda appealed to the Arizona Supreme Court, which affirmed the trial court's decision. He then appealed to the U.S. Supreme Court, which on a 5-4 vote reversed the state court's decision to allow the confession into evidence. The Court held that statements made by a defendant in response to police interrogation are admissible only if the defendant was informed of his right to an attorney and right to remain silent prior to questioning. It emphasized that Miranda was a particularly vulnerable interviewee due to being "seriously disturbed" and suffering from "emotional illness of schizophrenic type."

Miranda was retried on the original charges in 1967 and was convicted without the prosecution's use of the confession. He was paroled in 1972, but was in and out of prison over the next several years for various offenses. While free, he made a modest living working odd jobs and selling autographed Miranda Warning cards on the steps of the Phoenix courthouse. After several years of life on the fringes, he was stabbed to death in a fight. Several Miranda cards were found on him.

83

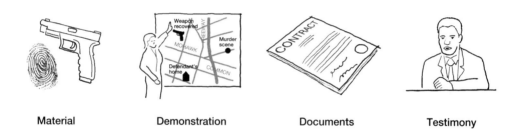

| Material | Demonstration | Documents | Testimony |

Common categories of evidence

Judge: "Am I never to hear the truth?"
Counsel: "No, my lord, merely the evidence."

—from Peter Murphy, *Practical Guide to Evidence*

84

Johnnie Cochran, criminal defense attorney

The integrity of the system is more important to the court than the truth of one case.

A trial's search for truth is invariably imperfect because it cannot be conducted in a way that introduces unfairness into the legal system. If a piece of evidence was improperly acquired or mishandled by the prosecution, it may be excluded from trial even if it provides an incontrovertible link between the defendant and the crime, because evidence in future cases could be similarly abused. If this allows a guilty person to go free, it is not because the court is not interested in the truth of the case; it is because it accepts that the truth must take some small lumps in the short run so the court gets better at finding the truth in the long run.

85

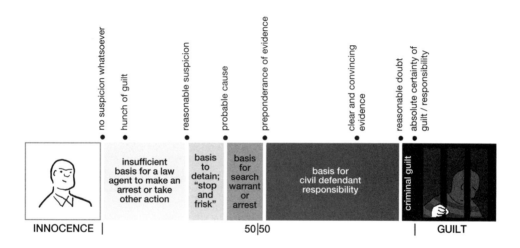

no suspicion whatsoever

hunch of guilt

reasonable suspicion

probable cause

preponderance of evidence

clear and convincing evidence

reasonable doubt

absolute certainty of guilt / responsibility

INNOCENCE

insufficient basis for a law agent to make an arrest or take other action

basis to detain; "stop and frisk"

basis for search warrant or arrest

50|50

basis for civil defendant responsibility

criminal guilt

GUILT

Standards of proof

Not guilty doesn't mean innocent.

In issuing a verdict of guilty, a jury asserts its belief that a criminal defendant is responsible for a crime beyond a reasonable doubt. A jury that believes a defendant is "probably guilty" must vote to acquit. A reasonable doubt must be derived rationally from the evidence, or from a lack of evidence presented by the prosecution. It cannot be based on sympathy for the accused, unfounded theorizing, or fanciful conjecture.

86

A judge trial might better suit:
- a case with complex legal questions
- a *pro se* (self-represented) litigant, as a judge might know to disregard irrelevant/ inflammatory evidence
- a large organization opposing a small organization or individual

A jury trial might better suit:
- a litigant whose case has a strong emotional component
- a personal injury litigant
- an individual or small organization opposing a large organization

A guilty verdict isn't binding.

A verdict is a jury's decision as to whether the facts presented to it fit the essential elements of a crime or civil harm. The judge uses the verdict as a guideline in creating an appropriate final judgment.

A judge may not overturn a verdict of not guilty. However, in most jurisdictions, judges can set aside a guilty verdict in a criminal case, or any verdict in a civil case, if they determine the jury reached its verdict in error or did not base it on sufficient evidentiary ground.

Objection, irrelevant.
The answer won't tend to prove or disprove a fact.

Objection, prejudicial.
The answer will mislead or confuse the jury.

Objection, speculation.
This witness lacks first-hand knowledge of the matter.

Objection, privileged.
My client does not have to reveal the confidences of her spouse.

Objection, hearsay.
The person to whom these remarks are attributed is not on the witness list.

Common objections

Winning the battle might not be worth the collateral damage.

Every case involves many small points of dispute: courtroom procedures, the admission of evidence, an inaccurate assertion by the opponent that, if refuted, may leave the jury confused, and more. Winning cases lose some of these battles. Size up quickly if a battle is worth fighting or if you should move on. Picking and losing too many battles can undermine your credibility before the court. It can also boost the confidence of your opponent, reducing the likelihood of a desirable settlement. And if a point of dispute is not central to your theory of the case, it likely will not work in your favor to engage it.

If overruled on a crucial point, however, request that your objection be put on the record in case you appeal the decision.

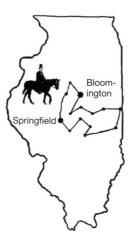

Federal judges once traveled the country on preset paths, or circuits, to hear cases.
Abraham Lincoln rode the circuit in Illinois. Circuits later became permanent districts.

Roe v. Wade, 410 U.S. 113 (1973)

Norma McCorvey, unsuccessful in her efforts to obtain an illegal abortion in Texas, sued the state of Texas in federal court, claiming state laws restricting abortion violated her right to privacy. The court ruled in favor of McCorvey (who used the alias Jane Roe) on the merits, but declined to issue an injunction that would have lifted the abortion ban.

On appeal by Roe, the U.S. Supreme Court, acting simultaneously on a companion case, *Doe v. Bolton*, ruled that the Constitution creates a right to personal privacy that extends to a woman's decision to have an abortion. However, the court balanced this right against the state's interest in guarding prenatal life and women's health by limiting state regulation to the third trimester of pregnancy. The Supreme Court later revised this limit to the point of fetal viability.

Roe v. Wade was a case of won battles and lost wars, or vice versa. Roe gave birth before the initial trial was complete. She won her case in district court but was not granted the injunction she desired. But the district court, despite not granting her the desired injunction, helped Roe fight a larger cause: its decision left room for the U.S. Supreme Court to issue a ruling with farther reaching force. In later decades, McCorvey came to regret her role in *Roe v. Wade* and became a pro-life advocate.

	for Bush (Republican)	for Gore (Democrat)
Appointed by Republican President		
Rehnquist	✔	
Scalia	✔	
Thomas	✔	
O'Connor	✔	
Kennedy	✔	
Souter		✔
Appointed by Democratic President		
Stevens		✔
Ginsburg		✔
Breyer		✔

Supreme Court Justices in *Bush v. Gore*, 531 U.S. 98 (2000)

Judges are biased.

Judges and juries interpret facts through the lenses of their own experiences. Although they may strive to be impartial, they cannot completely put aside their biases.

"We are under a Constitution, but the Constitution is what judges say it is."

—CHARLES EVANS HUGHES, U.S. Supreme Court Associate Justice (1910–1916) and Chief Justice (1930–1941)

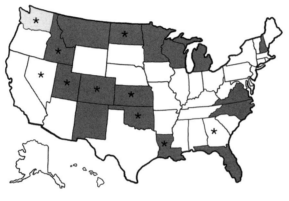

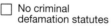 No criminal
defamation statutes

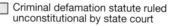 Criminal defamation statute ruled
unconstitutional by state court

■ Criminal statutes
against defamation

★ Criminal statutes against
defamation of the dead

States deliberately pass unconstitutional laws.

Many state statutes, such as those criminalizing sodomy or defamation, are on the books in the United States despite having been declared unconstitutional by the U.S. Supreme Court. A conviction made under them in state court likely would be overturned if appealed to the U.S. Supreme Court.

States sometimes pass **trigger laws** to express disagreement with the U.S. Supreme Court's interpretation of the Constitution. Such laws have a provision stating they will take effect (be triggered) if the Supreme Court changes its interpretation of the Constitution. A number of states have passed trigger laws to abolish abortion should the U.S. Supreme Court overturn its 1973 decision in *Roe v. Wade*.

92

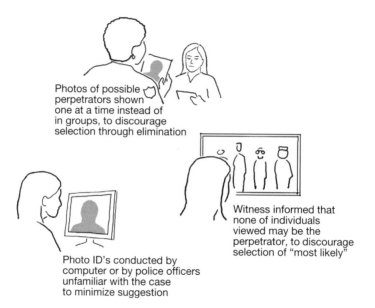

Photos of possible perpetrators shown one at a time instead of in groups, to discourage selection through elimination

Witness informed that none of individuals viewed may be the perpetrator, to discourage selection of "most likely"

Photo ID's conducted by computer or by police officers unfamiliar with the case to minimize suggestion

Some reforms in eyewitness identification

Memory is a crime scene.

According to the Innocence Project, more than three-fourths of convicts exonerated by DNA testing were found guilty on the basis of eyewitness testimony. Once thought highly accurate, eyewitness memory of an event is now known to be distorted by subsequent events, including the manner in which police conduct questioning, photo identifications, and line-ups. Like an unprotected crime scene, one's memory of a crime is a record that can be irrevocably altered by later events taking place in the same space.

Ronald Cotton and Jennifer Thompson

Ronald Cotton exoneration

Jennifer Thompson, a white college student, was attacked in her bed by an intruder. She carefully studied the rapist's features, and in a later photo lineup identified Ronald Cotton, an African American, as her attacker. Cotton, lacking a convincing alibi, was tried and convicted, and received a life sentence.

In prison, Cotton crossed paths with inmate Bobby Poole, to whom he bore a resemblance; guards and other inmates occasionally confused the two. Poole bragged that he had committed the crimes for which Cotton had been convicted. Cotton gained a retrial, but Thompson again identified Cotton as her attacker and did not recognize Poole, who was in the courtroom. Convicted of the Thompson rape again, as well as another rape also based on eyewitness identification, Cotton received a sentence of life plus 54 years.

Back in prison, Cotton contemplated killing Poole, who lived in the same dormitory, but was talked out of it by his father. Seven years after his second conviction, new lawyers for Cotton requested DNA review of the evidence. The only DNA sample left was a partial head of a sperm, but it was enough to prove conclusively that Poole, not Cotton, was the rapist. Ronald Cotton was freed after serving 10.5 years. Poole later died in prison.

Two years after Cotton's release, he and Thompson met and became close friends. They wrote a best-selling book about their experiences, and campaign together for reform in eyewitness testimony.

"We don't see things as they are, but as we are."

—ANAÏS NIN

Retributive justice
Focuses on satisfying the victim and
community by meting punishment in
proportion to the crime, the damage done,
or the benefit gained by the offender

Restorative or reparative justice
Focuses holistically on the needs of
victims, the community, and offenders,
who are asked to acknowledge, take
responsibility for, and repair harms

People act from a center of pain.

When in conflict, people rarely act from a rational, logical center. Otherwise reasonable individuals can distort the truth due to feelings of anger, fear, rejection, or frustration over being misunderstood. Often, varying accounts of a conflict can be reconciled without litigation by making sure each party fully hears the other side and is fully heard itself without interruption. Where accounts cannot be thus reconciled, people often will accept disagreement if they are certain they have been heard and understood, and they often will forgive wrongs when they know the reasons for them.

There never was a Twinkie defense.

San Francisco city supervisor Dan White, by many accounts, was an extraordinarily conscientious, well-respected member of his community. But in 1978, several days after resigning his position, White entered City Hall through an unguarded window and murdered Supervisor Harvey Milk and Mayor George Moscone. White's defense team did not deny his guilt, but claimed he had been severely depressed. He suffered from diminished mental capacity, it was argued, making him incapable of the premeditation required for first degree murder. A psychiatrist testified to the symptoms of White's depression, including a switch from a very healthy diet to one based on sugary snacks. The jury agreed that White's capacity was diminished, and convicted him of voluntary manslaughter. He received a seven-year sentence.

A tumultuous aftermath included public demonstrations and rioting, and the eventual abolition of the diminished capacity defense in California. A sarcastic reporter referred to White's defense as the "Twinkie defense." The phrase stuck, and it is still used to refer to an improbable or highly suspect defense tactic. However, no argument was made by White's lawyers that his diet caused him to commit the murders, only that it evidenced his depression.

97

"If only there were evil people somewhere insidiously committing evil deeds, and it were necessary only to separate them from the rest of us and destroy them. But the line dividing good and evil cuts through the heart of every human being. And who is willing to destroy a piece of his own heart?"

—ALEKSANDR SOLZHENITSYN
The Gulag Archipelago (1973)

98

The other students are scared, too.

Law school is tough for everyone, and law professors are often demanding and unclear. Owning your ignorance and asking questions are among your best tools for survival. The best questions to ask are often those you fear will make you appear stupid; the likelihood is high that other students will have the same questions. And perhaps as importantly, speaking up in class is good practice for speaking up in court.

99

You have to *find* a mentor; no one is going to make you a protégé.

It is unlikely anyone will seek you out to nurture your career, no matter how talented you are. Although many organizations have formal mentoring programs, a long-term mentor is usually someone you connect with over time on an intellectual and personal level.

You probably will have to do most of the work. Ask questions of those around you. Most people like to be asked for advice. Don't worry about their stature; a low-ranking associate could soon be a partner. But make your requests manageable; ask for input on specific issues. Save broad questions of career and legal philosophy for after hours.

100

Hillary Clinton
Secretary of State

Franz Kafka
Author

Mohandas Gandhi
Pacifist reformer

Robert Louis Stevenson
Author

Lisa Scottoline
Best-selling author

Alan Page
NFL Hall of Famer (MN Supreme Court Justice)

A career in law is continual preparation for a day that may never come.

Everything a lawyer does must be done with awareness of how it will hold up in a trial. Yet lawyers rarely get to argue in court. Even professional litigators spend little time in the courtroom, as over 90% of both criminal and civil cases are resolved prior to trial by plea bargain or settlement. Many suits are filed not with the goal of going to trial, but to prompt settlement by the other party.

A lawyer can't merely love being a showman in a public arena; a lawyer must love the law.

101

Notes

Lesson 2: Gallup, 2011

Lesson 21: LegalMetric, via "So Small a Town, So Many Patent Suits," *New York Times*, 24 September 2006

Lesson 54: American Bar Association and U.S. Census Bureau

Lesson 56: Nolo

Lesson 62: Court Statistics Project, 2009

Lesson 71: U.S. Department of Justice, U.S. Census Bureau, and Office of the Federal Register

Lesson 77: After the JD Project, American Bar Foundation

Index

Vibeke Norgaard Martin is an attorney in California. She practiced commercial litigation at a major international law firm before turning to civil rights litigation and criminal appeals. She has taught at the Boalt School of Law at the University of California, Berkeley, was a visiting scholar at the Centre for Child Law at the University of Pretoria in South Africa, and worked for the Sierra Leone Truth and Reconciliation Commission. Previously, she clerked for the South African Constitutional Court.

Matthew Frederick, an architect, is the author of *101 Things I Learned® in Architecture School* and the creator, editor, and illustrator of the 101 Things I Learned® series. He lives in Hudson, New York.

www.101thingsilearned.com